**Dining at the Edge**

Charles Freyberg

# Dining at the Edge

With special thanks to Judith Beveridge, Peter Urquhart, Tim Wright, Victor Sheehan, Danny Gentile, Sarah Gilbert, Kate Lilley, Richard Short, John O'Driscoll, Paul Scully, Alison Marshall, Charlotte Black, Martin Richardson, Troy Davies, Nadine Stransen, Mary Burgess, Patrick White, Candy Royalle, Lou Steer, Deirdre Freyberg and the poets of the University of Sydney poetry seminar for their inspiration, support and feedback.

*Dining at the Edge*
ISBN 978 1 76041 550 1
Copyright © text Charles Freyberg 2018
Cover image: painting by Martin Richardson
imposed on a photograph by Charles Freyberg

First published 2018 by
**GINNINDERRA PRESS**
PO Box 3461 Port Adelaide 5015
www.ginninderrapress.com.au

# Contents

| | |
|---|---|
| Buddha With Koto | 7 |
| Listening to Callas Sing Bellini at La Scala, 1952 | 9 |
| Lift | 11 |
| Saint Mark's Park, Bondi, 1980 | 15 |
| Haiku | 19 |
| Anaphora | 20 |
| Terrania Creek Fantasia | 21 |
| Goanna | 25 |
| Mist At Govett's Leap | 26 |
| Reflexivity | 28 |
| Love Song to Chelsea Manning | 31 |
| Taxi Driver in Paddington | 38 |
| Bewitched in the Park | 41 |
| Brown Eyes | 43 |
| Kings Cross 1973 Fantasia | 44 |
| Refuge For Romantics | 59 |
| Hospital Dance | 67 |
| To Nadine | 68 |
| Maria Barbola | 72 |
| Martin's Painting | 75 |
| Silver Birch Tree in China | 78 |
| 2014 | 81 |
| The Tickle | 91 |
| A Taunting Question in His Eyes… | 92 |
| Bruise | 98 |
| Oberon | 100 |
| To an Old Friend | 107 |
| Chick Corea's Crimson Sun in Brunswick | 112 |
| Pick Up | 116 |

# Buddha With Koto

Before I met you, I was a tourist,
but then I saw your fingers poised
on your bronze koto, a flower in your hair.
Are your eyes really closed? But I know they're aware:
You have a concentration, on the point of speaking
to a passerby like me, who wants to hear
a voice like yours. It sounds a little mad,
but I do hear it, first the tremor of a string,
and is it just the warm breath of summer wind
blowing through the legs of giant cedars
that have slowly grown and tottered
while you've been here, or words rising to song?
There's something that stays young in you –
your lips full, your fingers keen to play,
the bronze on your cheeks the green of new leaves,
passing to the worn dark of your priestly robe.
Now you're glowing in hot sun, but soon enough
there'll be blizzards, torrential rain, seasons
passing quickly with corrosive touch,
giving you the blotchy skin of a hermit,
alive to all the elements – do you sing of this?
Or perhaps of origami cranes and saki cups,
offerings to all the years of graves close by?
Do you see the moment each soul was
most alive, love suicides, planting a last kiss
on glowing skin, as they defy the pedants, sharing death?
Mutilated soldiers, flying high on the wings of cranes
folded by their children – or lives that last
until dementia, still raving of a schoolyard prank?

Your voice is agile, undulating in exploration,
moments exploding and passing with wild variation.
The first leaves on a seedling sprout
as some mighty trunk crashes.
You're a wise old gossip, a gentle young man
torn by disappointment, but standing firm
you find a stubborn balance, an ironic voice
that cracks with emotion, then quietens
with reflection, sharply plucking strings.

# Listening to Callas Sing Bellini at La Scala, 1952

You sigh, picking at the scab
of a wound deep inside you.
The blood flows in a single tear.
Smoke blows from my mouth,
drifting in the form of a lost lover
over plates and bottles, then he fades,
leaving you and me. We stare far away.
The room tilts as a blood-red glass
crashes to the floor, and I reach
for *her*, knowing she understands,
revolving warped on vinyl that's been
everywhere I have and survived,
gathering cracks.
You know how far gone I am
whenever I need to hear her.
She's like an obsession, squirming alone
on sweaty sheets – she embroiders
her guts with a knife for a needle.
So we are not alone,
as she reaches into her enraged diaphragm
for longing rolls of resignation,
questioning and rising to an answer
in a pitch that excruciates,
jangling from her breath to ours,
tearing our mouths open in a gasp
that quivers, splintering alongside
her exquisitely trained trills.

As she pauses, cellos brood over
this private moment twisting with bass
and baritone harmony, and we wait for her,
standing and mouthing her defiance
as gowns and coloured lights flicker
on our bodies instead of just T-shirts,
turning any lingering of sadness
into something like Callas, singing
at a crumbling La Scala. Eyes glow,
and emaciated bodies breath more deeply now,
as we sing with her in the ruins
of a war that's over at last.
I see your body inflate with her emotion
as she gallops sweating blood
like a thoroughbred,
cascading in a resounding canter
ever faster to her shattering
high note.
Silence.
Applause? Stamping? Brava! Brava!?
Not quite. Just a cracked needle.
We are bewildered.
Greasy dinner plates, almost empty bottles.
I pour and we drink,
suddenly choking in crazy laughter.
Can we ever train our pain
and wonder to weave an illusion
as rich as this? Rest well, Maria

# Lift

My scarlet glove
presses the worn handle.
Murmuring chains
fall silent with a snap.
Iron lattices part.
The cabin quivers to a halt,
then the hiss of doors like scorn.

I gasp a warm breath in
from the marble lobby's bustle,
then the chatter of a trolley tripping
along the gleaming surface.
Bags dwarf the bell boy,
their leather bellies bursting,
as hands brush snowflakes
off quilted tweed, and back and forth
words comfortably drone and sigh.
A droplet falls on shining leather.

My glove flicks the handle,
the geometry of iron springs back.
The floor, a fading fleur-de-lis
jolts, as pulleys heave,
the chains whine and whisper.
The button punctured leather cabin
stinks of goulash and liqueur.
The bags shake, then laughter
at a joke I've heard in many voices.

I sit unnoticed, woollen backsides
hem me in, I hold my breath...
...until she's next to me,
always bright in silken blue
with frayed green feathers,
a little like my scarlet vest,
my pompommed cap with its fleur-de-lis...

Glove on handle, a hiss like scorn,
then a warm breath in
from the turquoise carpeted corridor.
Bags, coats and patchouli jostle
away to their starched sheets
and feathered oak beds.

I wonder how I came to be here.
I'm alone, I chuckle,
as the other lift clangs by,
the generator hums,
stoked and stoked with coal.
Warm air wafts
up the shaft from the bowels below.
I shiver, wiping away beads of sweat.

Rain crackles with fire
as the mud explodes,
ripping nerves into tatters…
the bell is clanging
chains screech,
a breath of warm air,
castanets of shoes march
over the lobby's marble.

She's with me again,
pale in her feathers,
fingers like clock hands
circle cheeks with blush.
Her eyes are dark,
with a shimmer, a glimpse
beyond the bragging surfaces.
She never speaks
but sometimes
in a wonderful moment of silence
she looks at me and smiles.
Then she vanishes,
then the bell like a gong.

Three stumbling greatcoats
covered with snowflakes
exhale their brandy and jokes…
In an hour she will return
breathless, clock-hand fingers
wiping away the blush.
That hint of laughter in her eyes
at the rigmarole we share!
I want to speak,
but I do not desire.
Flying metal tore it away…
'Floor *Four*, you dolt!'
'Begging your pardon, sir!'
The doors hiss like scorn.

The screws at my knee are loose,
I feel a stab of pain
exploding with the bell.
Will I pick up my crutches
and limp into the open sky
above the street on this wintry night?

# Saint Mark's Park, Bondi, 1980

1

With the set smile of a puppet,
he bids us all good night – the *7.30 Report*
fades to blackness and all is silent.
I'm sitting in idleness waiting for a spark.
I feel a spite for chat of well spent days,
all my records scratched in favourite places,
I crush my foot on a novel's spine,
these surfaces so flimsy – and I wait,
knowing it's there – I'm teased by a shadow,
grabbing, setting hair on end, thrilling my body.
I free myself from drowning in the couch,
and leap out of the walls and fragile
surface of order – that is my home.

## 2 Bondi Beach

I feel the promise now, my pace increasing
I hear a rushing muffled rumble
in the fading light of the last houses.
Yet I'm tapped and tapped by a warning niggling –
a friends whisper, stifled to a worried look
by dancing bodies in a bar, then I turn and see
a gently bearded boy strumming a guitar,
dark curls in the wind, voice soaring,
then turned to mime by each wave crashing.
My body draws back – I'm blinded by the night,
my pace now taut as I press on down the path,
my home now distant, flickering with candlelight.

Sinews flex as the waves gather, swell
then topple. I'm glad to be alone.
The water recedes and darkens
to black blue tinged and ruffled,
until it folds into the sky, its pitch
a softer texture, buoyant and weightless.
I search for the point the elements meet,
but they jostle in the murk and it eludes me.
The wind suddenly hits me
with the tang of sea spray
from breakers exploding on rocks,
the foam is swallowed back,
dragged deeply under, making the next waves jump,
torn out of shape, charged with more tension,
their line broken with choppy plumes.
I feel my breath touch my guts
then escape in a gasp – I know it's there –
this massive force, pushing and pulling
far underneath, forming and breaking the pattern.

I see a man walking – I retreat into shadow,
then feel the push in my body and follow.
Ahead are the cliffs, brooding in stillness
like weathered faces in a mausoleum,
they stare with no eyes, as *my* pupils dilate.
There's no one source for their weird scrutiny,
just a hugeness, mottled and glowing.
I climb a winding set of stairs
hewn from rock, the park is at the top.
I will be ready – for whatever it reveals.

## 3 St Mark's Park

The wind shakes bushes in circles like water,
its voice ebbs and flows, waves pound in its silence,
then a long note reaching up past hearing.
Rubbish hops and rests on the grass.
The stranger is gone – no one is here,
except – there is a shadow – it flickers
in alertness as it draws another to it.
My eye zooms to each tiny gesture.
Hunched shoulders relax to openness,
they enfold, joining, then they separate –
a micron turning, wavering head he has sensed me!
Blushing invisibly I follow them.
Smell of sweat mingles with sea spray
just behind that rock, the saliva
on a lashing tongue, bodies merge with stone,
I cannot join. I am quite alone,
no longer wound into wind and waves,
alone, but not proud, full of wanting and doubt,
I crouch behind a shrub and shiver.
Then I see *him*, arms enwrapped,
senses torn, jangling, like mine,
dark curls blowing, body sad in waiting.
I will unwrap him and he will me,
nestling in my tenderness, the pulsing
of his naked chest, delicate then grabbing,
his face now rising, his lips poised but no speech,
eyes asking, glowing then closing…
I glide to him from behind,
touch his shoulder, bigger, stronger
than I thought, and when he turns

his face! Eyes lash me like a broken bottle,
pupils explode in flashing, empty blue.
His hand grabs my throat, and I choke
out the others – three, four.
I'm torn to the ground, dragged along,
they're circling, kicking, spewing fuck
from mouths that hardly open.
They are swathed in blackness – nothing else,
unlike sea and air, layered with shadows
of dark possibility – they are just blackness,
kicking, spitting, pulling tufts of hair,
as they lift me high, past stinking breath
and laughter – as I look out and see
that fold between sky and ocean close.

4

He sees it as he jogs in dawn's thin light,
a body in limbo, washed onto the rocks,
then sucked back out, striking them again,
before disappearing, reappearing
like a fantasy of medieval torture.
It rises again and he glimpses the face
the eyes wide open, tip of nose, the rest blue gash.
Yet the essence is there – he knows him –
Where? Startled eyes leap, fall away again
as he crouches and retches – his glance at a bar,
his body in shadow in the park above –
one night he spent there before he heard
a friend's whispered warning. He looks up at the cliffs…

This poem is dedicated to over thirty gay men who were murdered
near St Mark's Park, South Bondi, between 1975 and 1990.

# Haiku

Your hand beckons
Hair blowing in the wind
Laughter joining sunshine

# Anaphora

Against the chorus,
>My notes are wrong.
In the shouting and braying,
>I go silent.
When everyone knows,
>I don't have a clue.
The newest device
>Is tired and trashy.
Forgotten books,
>Are full of spontaneity.

Amongst the neurotic,
>I make sense.
When I bow,
>I find dignity.
In the silence,
>Violas and oboes.
In times of confusion,
>I find the answers.
When I can't write,
>My brain is teeming.

Amongst the rich dishes,
>It's you I hunger for.
When you don't notice,
>I see it all.
So throw me a bone –
>I will throw it back.
When I want to belong,
>I show my perversity.

# Terrania Creek Fantasia

'So overpowering was the draw of these trees that people risked their lives. A spirit of transformation emanated from the forest.'
Ian Cohen, Greens MLC, 1997

A raindrop's coldness
clings to my cheek
then scatters to the breeze.
My eyes twist along
a jagged fallen tree trunk
torn open to reveal
a swirling of rings inside
an autobiography
turning to mulch, eaten by moss,
a circling of faces half-forgotten
as a chatter breaks the drizzly silence.
Your face is the last, dear friend,
a loop of your words repeating
like drops of rain
searching for gaps in my coat,
their chill settles on my body's warmth.
I try to squirm
as they enter me more deeply.

I got in a car.
I drove away.
Freeway, highway, town, fields –
until a signpost
a dirt road narrowing,
led me to this towering forest.
I searched for a place to enter –
a chink, a path…

Inside the trunk's sodden roughness,
lines meander wildly
unique as my thumbprint.
The pattern is the same – or does it change
just a little with each repetition?
Branches break away, bending,
almost ready to writhe,
until they disappear
into a strangle of vines
each leaf a variation on a heart
heavy with droplets
that glisten grey as spots of light
squeeze through the waving canopy.
The crack of a whipbird, then another,
unseen like the burping frogs.
Almost silence, just the breeze's whisper
as you stare at me from the shadows,
and a brief smile of sunlight
dapples the crazy sculptured trunk.
Words joust again in a hiss of static.
My lungs hurt
as I draw on a cigarette.
A whipbird cracks,
the frogs are blowing raspberries.

I got in a car.
I drove out of the city.
The dirt road narrowed.
I found a chink
to enter this towering forest.
I walk on.

My smoke drifts in sunlight
as water pooled above
gathers through a gap in rock and falls
churning and pausing, pooling anew –
almost still, a moment of clarity
over pebbles rounded and shining like pearls
except for frothy circles
spreading larger as they spin,
expanding and vanishing
so quickly they're always there,
renewing and repeating, larger and smaller,
a whisper against the water whooshing
through endlessly polished scales of brown,
a glimpse inside the rock's black surface.
And always, like a distant drumming,
the sound of the nearby falls –
I look up and search for them in vain
as a whipbird cracks, the frogs burp.
I find instead a tree's gigantic trunk
and follow it,
past staghorns, the scars of branches lost,
skipping shadows of leaves above,
as a bird swoops out of layers of fern fronds.
The creek's voices are bubbling together
like a choristers scattered far and wide –
hums, whispers and basses,
a language that cannot be spoken,
but full of such patterns of feeling,
I begin to know what it's saying.

Circles bubble on the pool
as I sense you beside me,
slowly breathing like me.
Then you vanish,
except for your breath and thoughtfulness.

I rise to my feet…

# Goanna

The moment I see that texture
glistening from mud and leaves, sucking in
their colour, as the track widens in a stream

of sunlight, my panting breath slows
almost to the stillness of a speckled goanna
basking on the path, alive.

Black curve streaked with yellow,
his spine twists long from crocodile head
to the bulge of his well fed torso,

and just as I gasp
at the marvel of his presence,
a shock of breath inflates his scaly skin,

quivering through his stumpy limbs –
leaves and mud crackle.
Then he pauses and yawns,

his mouth gapes in delicate pink,
a blue worm of tongue shooting out,
then he scuttles away, twisting

through echoing undergrowth. I move away,
clambering awkward over a rock, wishing back
that long moment of goanna stillness.

## Mist At Govett's Leap

It's August chill:
cold hands warming
slowly to my touch,
your body opens to the valley,
surprised like your eyes.

Droplets sweat and bob
in the cool
of a lethargic breeze,
too tiny to wet
our enlivened cheeks,
but enough in their billions
to cover the valley
in a shroud of thick white light.

Leaves circle,
receding in focus
as the mist deepens
tingeing with colours
as my mind's eye
reaches past
the last tree's shadow
into the blue/green leap.
I try to remake
a faraway rock-
still surely there,
a castle-like absurdity.
You are close
beside me jauntily
delighted,
but my eyes revolve.

Everything I know
is well beyond
this damp air
turning solid
in a kind of pearly
midday night.

I turn
and see you standing still
in raptness.
What? what?
You touch your lips
then point
to the edge of vision
where a black cockatoo
preens on a branch
sharp
even to the white tip of its tail
flirting outrageous
against the deepening mist,
now blinding with sunlight.
Feathers bunch
gathering warmth
as it opens its wings
and flies,
momentarily scattering
the droplets around it.
The branch still shakes
as it disappears.

# Reflexivity

to accompany a viola sonata by Peter Urquhart

The lake gleams
in the muffled sunlight,
its surface,
a rippling wafer of silk,
peels away to reveal
a forest shimmering in the breeze.

Tree trunks ooze
with moss and feather fern,
under fresh leaves shaking-
a sharpness blurring to a haze
climbing up the jagged hill.

Smudges of grey
like rags squeezed out
float over clouds
in downy white
puffed like a seabird's throat.

A lapping at my feet,
a tangle of lily stems
shoots with a jewellery
of needles and flowers.

A glowing greenness,
laced with grey smudges
in a foam of downy white,
reaches deep into the water's dark,
like a painting from some age of vividness.

I see under the wings
of a bird hovering,
then it dives
a splash on the ghostly surface.

Tree tops shimmer, leaves
falling to a blur down the jagged hill,
until a fold at the edge of the lake, then
a second towering forest rises,
hazing faraway in layers of emerald,
shrouded in cloud,
rippling in water towards me.

Is it a copy, or a photograph
emerging from a bath,
a million year exposure?
I see my own shape,
standing tall and swaying in wonder,
wrapped in lilies at the water's edge.

Then the sun bursts glaring from the clouds,
the images fade,
the lake's depths shrouded
in silken blue blackness,
ruffling in the breeze.

So I take these images to you,
faint memory exploding with imagination,
hoping to see the reflection in your eyes.

Was it an uncanniness of light,
after a gentle shower in summer,
revealing the lake's hidden memory?

# Love Song to Chelsea Manning

*US Marines on R&R, Fitzroy Gardens near Kings Cross, Sydney, 2013*

Crew cuts with glowing faces.
Trained muscles energise the fabric
of matching uniforms, thick wrists
with fancy silver watches. It's like they're hunting,
joined by a thread of common breath,
knitting them in a cluster.
Voices rumble deep with shrillness,
listening and watching – to dump their tension,
bar first, then a brothel…
I look up from my book,
beneath my favourite tree exhaling smoke,
bristling and excited by their intrusion.
I see you walk between them.
You irritate their tempo
with your singularity,
setting off a fury.
They don't look you in the eye!
They try to tame your seeming smallness,
dragging you by a twisted arm…

*…to your court martial in Washington*!

Chelsea –
I see you on the news,
impeccable in dress uniform
between their contemptuous hands,
head no higher than their shoulders,
walking like a heretic
about to be tied at the scaffold.

Your face gaunt, awkward glasses
slightly askew on shaved temples
pulsing with thought, your blue eyes
calm, looking far away with resignation.
Cuffed hands nestle to
your solar plexus, touching a tremor
tearing through the creases of
your uniform – you joined to blot it out –
to be one of them!

Did you see them pass once
and feel the same as me?
Repulsive attraction –
wanting to wear their mask
of hearty thoughtlessness?
Or did you want to knock them to the ground,
and make them beg in a pretty Southern squeal?

*He was unique, extremely unique. Very quirky, very opinionated, very political, very clever, very articulate.*
A schoolfriend at Tasker Millward School, Wales

*He was barely five foot. A runt, so pick on him. Crazy, pick on him. A faggot, pick on him. He took it from every side. If the drill sergeants screamed at him, he would scream back.*
A fellow recruit at Fort Leonard Training Camp, Missouri

*Saint Paul's College, University of Sydney, 1983*

It was an all male college. I was 18. He was friendly with the football jocks, and I was besotted with him. I was alone with him walking back from the pub one night. I suddenly started kissing him. He pushed me away. Later that night, I heard them coming. I locked my door. They tried to break it down. They poured a tub of urine mixed with vomit underneath it. I heard a scratching on the door. When they went away, I had a look. They'd cut 'poofter' into the wood with a knife.

*A cupboard at Forward Base Hammer near Baghdad, 2008*

I lie here in a ball,
to protect all I see and think
wrapped up in my uniform.
I want! I take a knife and
cut it in the vinyl of
a chair – where I sit for
fourteen hours a day, fourteen hours
jumping from link to link in
the secret brain of who we are.
Who I am? There's something
so full, so strong and precocious,
taking shape in me – as I seethe
with all that happens
behind our public face,
the endless screens of bitter images.
My colleagues drink to unwind,
I can only do this. I hug the chair.
I loosen my shirt and breathe.
I'm finding myself here…

*US Army helicopter crew on reconnaissance in Baghdad, 2008*

*26 Buckmaster to Hotel 67*
*Five to six individuals with AK47s.*
*Request permission to engage.*
*They're behind the building.*
*Goddammit.*
*Line 'em up.*
*Shoot.*
*Keep shootn'*
*Keep shootn'*
*You shoot I'll talk.*
*We got one crawling down there.*
*All you gotta do is pick up a gun, buddy.*
*Oh yeah! Look at all them dead bastards.*
*Nice. Nice.*
*Good shootn'*
*Thank you.*
*We have a blue bongo truck picking up bodies.*
*Request permission to engage.*
*I lost 'em in the dust.*
*Look at that. Right through the windshield.*
*Ha Ha!*
*Serves them right, bringing their children with them into battle.*

*Forward Base Hammer. Army Intelligence IT Room*

I hear their voices
Deep. Shrill. Self-satisfied.
Like I hear them laughing in a bar
at some joke I can't understand.
Eight men – one with a long lense camera.
Blue truck with children stops to help
Hail of bullets falling bodies plumes of dust.
They have no idea. Out of their depth here,
like me. Full of anxiety at every turn,
like me. They find joy in murder,
but me? Now I see things clearly.
I save it to my disk.
It's ready –
The truth behind our posturing,
all our scorn and brittleness.
I've gathered it piece by piece
as I dive below
the surface of our global masquerade.
Someone must see this!
'We all must debate this,
Or we're gone as a species',
I type this like I'm whispering
to a cryptic portal which does not even
ask my name! The icon hovers over 'send'.
I press the button, and it's gone.
I look up. I breathe.
All around me monitors glow,
hushed choruses of chatter.
My loneliness is terrible…

*Torture to me is what the terrorists did on 9/11… Our objective is to get the guys who did 9/11, and to avoid another attack on the United States.*
Dick Cheney, former vice president, in an interview with Chuck Todd in *The Atlantic*, December 2014

*Military Prison at Marine Corps Base, Quantico, Virginia, 2009*

'Look left!' I look right.
'Look right!' I look left.
Eyes at the tiny window of my cell,
Mocking
in concern that I will end it all.
I am naked,
so all *they* can see
is my small, featureless body.
But it's just an outer frame,
a bad draft for something fuller.
Just a little of my crushed passion
makes my gaunt skull teem
with blondness, thin lips
purple and full for kissing,
sagging ribs inflate with
my rich seductive laughter.
Could I really hang
from my underpants and flip-flops?
They've taken them too!
I followed them dumbly
when I only had the courage to be a man.
How stupid are they, moving jerkily

like robots with one breath between them!
A woman – Submissive? – not me, them!
As a woman I can understand,
I assembled the truth piece by piece,
within their blundering I found my mind –
Quirky, uncompromising, a terrifying energy.
I want to wear an explosive dress,
blown by the wind in a crowded street,
firing my lover's wild imagination.
And yet – those eyes at the window,
'Look left! Look right!'
every five minutes!
'I WANT MY FLIP-FLOPS!"
Silence. My thin formless body. Silence.

Thank you, Chelsea Manning. I love you xxxx Charles Freyberg

# Taxi Driver in Paddington

Always moving,
sitting in one place.
I scan the pavement for a hand.
The road curves and widens.
Brake lights flash
as a brooding bass swells.
I turn it up and hum.
*The Dutchman* sails on,
flying, cursed! He cannot land
until he finds… How I loved
the smell of your skin, fresh from the shower,
a glimpse of red freckles…
The road repeats itself,
round every corner.
The terraces shed layers of paint,
a guitar riff blurs,
your Che Guavara poster
is Blu-tacked to the wall.
I drink from a cup
stained with cask wine,
you're dancing
as I squeeze the last for you…
As Wagner yearns,
your freckles are gone.
Buildings replicate, flashing by –
all flaws removed,
surfaces freshly manicured,
floodlit like a deserted film set,
the blackness of midnight above.

Nobody!
A horn sounds.
I scan the pavement for a hand
as the road continues glistening.

Always moving,
sitting in one place.
Three bangs echo.
Voices sprawl together.
A flash of blonde hair.
Hawaiian shirt screeches.
I warmly imagine
some misfit they're laughing at.
Bodies crackle, shrill energy
without context. Their music
bangs and bellows, clinging, clinging
to the present right in my face,
my brooding bass was shit
they quickly silenced.
And yet – they're faraway,
like the city slowly passing,
washed out and flat.
I retreat and become
the brown curve of the console,
the coloured glow from a smear
on the windscreen, the change of gears
as water cools my heat.
I sigh. Red freckles, narrow street,
road veers and widens. I change the channel,
massed choir – what happened to that restaurant?

How I loved your smell…but the road
takes over, I scan the pavement for a hand.
I am scattered, thoughts repeat in fragments
like the city. I can't get out.
Always moving,
sitting in one place.

# Bewitched in the Park

Your largeness and laughter
are at home here, sprawled in the grass.
Some hungry pigeons are listening too.
Soon witches awake – clouds blush,
smudged with haze, bent in the branches –
a time for storytelling, lounging in the park.

You tell a break-up well,
the first encounter blissful,
but it quickly descends,
as your lover stumbles with awfulness,
and our laughter joins in hooting harshness,
then a silence when I see your sadness,
and you see mine…

Raising an eyebrow, I flick it away,
and paint you a gorgeous bully
I once was besotted with, and as you listen
you sweep back long disordered hair,
like Mother Earth chuckling in the grass,
hippy boy with Gothic shadows
under eyes glinting with waywardness,
your cheekbones glow, no longer jaded –
my story finds its zest from you.

Ragged with brightness,
I see you lip synching,
Kate in wuthering blustering moors,
'Lover man, oh where can you be?'
then mouth wide open, astonishing high note,
lyrics patchy, but we capture the feeling.

What now for you?
What now for me?
I kissed you – more than once,
but that was then, and I know you.
Your head is on my shoulder,
like there's a sudden downpour
you need shelter from…
You're on the point of taking off,
always between things
without a home,
that's why I seek you,
poised in your aloneness
but I can't grasp you.

The pigeons are gone.
We leave as shadows lengthen.
On the street outside,
I see your awkwardness,
perhaps you see mine,
amongst the bustling couples.
You're outside it.
Unlike me, you don't mask it.

# Brown Eyes

You do not always speak in words,
but from the depth of your brown eyes.
They resist my stare, I look away,
I cannot read them and so I sigh.
Then as I quickly glance again
at you, so near, looking inward,
as I pour the warmth of more red wine,
the silence of your eyes is lush with thought,
brightening, still with a hint of darkness,
which is how I feel, and suddenly
your thankful smile, that I return,
grows into your laughter, a resounding
leap of it, unlike anyone else's.
And somehow those phantoms
hissing from the past are changed –
into big children, stumbling like us,
kicking us alive. The story of
an engaging clown looking for love,
about to slip on a banana skin
everyone else can see – he falls
sheds tears, dusts himself, and looks again.
We laugh at ourselves and each other –
it's all from another life, feeding this one.
The last shreds of dinner glisten
as Leonard Cohen's love song fades.
You look at me, touch my shoulder, laugh again,
as perhaps you, or me launches another story.
An oboe gyrates, asking a lively question.
I pour you a wine, we survived it all,
more than survived, we're flourishing!
I'm looking again into your brown eyes.

# Kings Cross 1973 Fantasia

## Michael in the Suburbs

It's no longer my room,
it belongs to my double.
For years he slept in my body.
He absently walked the tree lined avenue.
The worlds he explored were always far away,
a voyeur of ancient tragedy,
of obsolete maps and family trees.
I always knew it was not enough.
My sister and parents are sleeping,
but I can not.
I take off my greasy waiter's shirt –
what would Raskalnikov think?
I lie on my childhood bed,
eiderdown blue, embroidered with cars.
I fling it away,
squirming in gorgeous nakedness.
Beyond the billowing curtains
are rows of dark houses, secretly dreaming.
This a home for him, but not for me,
as his law books reproach me on the shelf,
and my body explodes with caresses
it can never find here.
I reach for the cassette and stare into
the shine of humorous eyes,
the wild mop of curls on the wall.
'the answer is blowing in the wind'.

## Louise in the Suburbs

I cook by rote,
the meat is dry,
our eyes drained of colour
like the vegies, all flavour gone.
His red wine nauseates,
his sentences finish in my head,
the moment his grumbling starts,
an endless chewing of gristle,
an echo of his dried up friends,
as he trails off and stares.
I've forgotten how to love,
I know the clammy coldness
of his next touch and his next,
he's drained to a tiresome shadow of himself.
I wanted to gather some fiery collage
from books dead on the shelf behind him,
our thoughts stepping in crescendo
towards some astonishing newness.
Now I only mutter as I ask to leave the table,
to sit in the chilly darkness of our bedroom,
encircled by his brooding, and he in mine.

## Car Job

Vanessa at the Wall, Darlinghurst

I shiver under the streetlight
just to show some enticing flesh,
bitten by the winter breeze,
dreaming of pavlova with strawberries and cream.
My shawl is transparent, in scarlet lace,
now damp and soiled at the edges.
Others preen at the edge of shadow,
our craving clusters us,
drives us apart,
vying to be seen,
our acid gossip quickly shifts
to nail flailing fury
if you cross the line.
We wait for a car,
tensely jostling for space
against a sandstone wall
which if you stop to listen
still rattles with the breath
of prisoners fighting and flirting there before us,
a gathering of the thwarted.

A car slows,
shaking with anticipation,
a plume of warm exhaust.
I stand nonchalant,
I tingle with his scrutiny,
a shadowy telepathy of wanting,
I know he's picked me.

Does a fumble at the door latch
break the spell I'm casting?
Squeaking vinyl as he shifts,
my foot rests on a smiling doll,
I touch a quivering hand
as his body twists,
with a caress, I slap him away.
A crumpled note, I ask for triple,
I glisten in his pleading eyes,
the doll's face squawks a laugh,
I'm his lost youth, his freedom.
Springing from a cage in the suburbs,
a whipped little man asserts himself,
ripping at my dress, touching flesh,
it must be now, an unlit side street,
then he unzips, reaching for my head.

My shaking hands contort behind me,
searching for the eyelets on my blouse,
so I can return to my silken composure,
floating high above, milking men's lust.
I light a cigarette,
on the periphery, the others smirk –
I cannot ask their help.
My broken bloody body
will soon rest in some dumpster.

I'm a lost boy, dishevelled,
looking for gentle hands to help,
a freakish soul to laugh with
at my trick's feeble grunt,
then his rage
as he pushed me from the car
cursing clawing for his cash,
my heart still thumping,
he bruised me as I punched him,
my beauty no protection
but I find a little calm
reaching for my lipstick.

There are colourful lights
at the bottom of the tunnel,
glowing at the end of the street.
I walk from the cackle of hanged men,
towards a new chaos of possibility,
the wild flirtation of cafes and bars.
I play with the notes,
and there's more if I stand again.
Oh never again!
I can dance,
or bewitch my admirers with my idle thoughts.
And yet…I'm addicted
to the rush of adrenalin images.

## Michael on Darlinghurst Road

I move through ever changing light,
as jumping pig and pussycat
cast an alluring red
tinged with green
over clusters of searching faces,
but I cannot settle on anyone
as shoes jostle, swerving on asphalt.
A seagull squawks at chips in the gutter.
Love songs intertwine
from each new door
in blue and purple balls of light,
glowing in the bubble of schooners.
Drinkers pulsate, gesturing and dancing.
Faces jump out from the rev of cars honking.

I'm here for myself,
not trapped in a tightening, unloving knot of men,
with clenched arms and ogling faces.
The checks in the starch of my shirt
are circling, jumping,
so far away from my room's dull truth
of static white light.
I'm revolted, I'm electric,
I want to run home
but I open my arms
and let it all shake me,
as a handsome drunk
knocks me off my feet,
and smiles as he scuttles away.

I look up from dodging boots and stilettoes.
Tree leaves flutter with pinkness
as the cat's purple tongue licks its green whiskers.
It stretches and jumps, then gives me a wink.
I'm here, I'm alone
as love twists high in guitar and song,
boy fights with girl as engines screech.
I'm alone with all this,
not the reproach of dark voices,
and my eiderdown in baby blue
embroidered with cars.

## Tony and the Boss at the Venus Room

The Venus is jumping,
the girls all legs in minis,
trays of glowing amber with ice,
low light from a chandelier,
shadows of men stumble with bravado.
The boss arrives,
sitting at his centre table,
the potency
of his jovial stare
tears inhibitions, notes fly from wallets,
the revelry intensifies,
animal shouts over jazz band jive.

Knowing he is watching,
I circle and smile,
adjusting the buttons of my scarlet suit,
flaunting its muscular line.

I keep the moment electric,
spiralling not quite out of control,
with a wink, a handshake, a threat,
ready for a flying fist, a broken off glass,
as girls hustle men to softly furnished rooms.

He beckons.
He wants me.
I sit, his eyes opaque stare playfully into mine.
'His dirty fingers in the till…'
He pauses as a waitress giggles,
bringing us whiskies and ice…
'You know what to do.'
The quiet insinuation in his voice
cuts through the bellowing music,
as the bar revolves around him,
sweeping in cops who jump when he says,
he sits easy,
fury wrapped in his well cut suit,
easing into a chuckle as he jokes,
a Walther bulges from his coat,
he's ready to pounce at any intruder,
he came from nothing like me.
Now the Premier invites him to lunch.
'Yes, boss.'
He trusts me.
I leave with a skip,
shaking with a dread that makes me stronger.

# A Café in Roslyn Street

Louise

I sit on the edge,
as wide eyed boys play guitar,
street girls wipe the purple from their lips.
Thoughts fly high,
wrapped in sudden contagious laughter,
from long hair and spectacles,
colourful bodies swivel and gesture,
then a silence,
but before I can speak,
some new speculation glows,
taking shape amongst them,
so I listen,
fearing the tremble of my voice
amongst people so unlike me,
so comfortable in themselves.
A line of drunks stumble by exhausted,
tied together like a chain gang.
Above in the darkest patch of night,
his finger slowly motions,
his voice flat with certainty,
'Come back. Who are these people?
You're not well, but I love you.
Let me explain the world to you.'
And just as I agree,
I see an orange slither in the sky,
fresh dew in the wintry breeze.

I see him, I see her,
overdone make-up reddening her eyes,
or is it tears,
is she chatting with demons like me?
She becomes still, a beat
and suddenly we breath together
in something as strange as laughter.
I choke on my cigarette,
surprised at myself at last.

## Vanessa and Tony

Naked in silence
I caress
the slash of a scar
poking from your chest hair,
rough pinkness like stitching
expands with your ribs as you snore.
My sequins and taffeta
neatly folded on a chair,
your suit scattered, now unsuave,
a butt yellow-tars your cotton shirt.
There's only my body now and yours,
still sweating on your rumpled sheets.
I'm dizzy in the vodka's bitter reek,
as the cut knuckles of your hand
gently rest on my breast.
I kiss your imperfections.

# Michael on Darlinghurst Road
## Reflections in Rhinestone

Waistcoats hand in hand with frocks,
sailors lurching arm in arm,
they all rush by
as I pause, a moment to breathe.

Only then do I see
laughter in rolling eyes,
flowing beard in tangles,
his cape a dirty blanket,
coins in a hat at blistered feet.

He sits on a bank's granite steps,
our faces reflect on rails of polished brass.
I reach into my pocket,
but he shakes his grey head,
he welcomes me as I sit by him.

He wears a rhinestone necklace,
balls of sparkling prisms
flashing in an aura of red and blue.
'We spin off our axis,
we crash and we burn.'

A foreign accent – a knowing
rhythm from Europe's darkness.
Mocking men, blue eyed in a pack,
kick at his cap of coins,
scattering, clattering on black,
they spin then they fall…

…they knock me to the ground and kick me
in a sunny playground,
bloody lips shocked to numbness,
my head smashing on asphalt…

…I like his blanket's pungency
as I lean into its warmth.
He touches my cheek, ruffles my hair,
my throat burns as I sip from his bottle.

He gives me a rhinestone,
and in its multifaceted reflection,
my face shifts bewildered into gorgeousness.
'It's your to keep till the end of the world.'
His smile is a reflection of mine.
I'm finding the future in rhinestone.

## Vanessa and Tony 2

The city is ours,
framed in your window.
Shadowy buildings
with pinpricks of light
ride on the black
of the harbour's ink,
thickening like treacle.

I start to sink.
You are writhing,
coloured figments jostle
on your sleeping lids,
your scar is tearing,
weeping blood and pus,
or is it mine?

Rocking in the grey hush above us,
I see a frightened boy –
is it you? No, it's me –
hanging dresses touch his body
wrapped in a ball –
he's hiding in a wardrobe,
from…

Spittle from a mouth wide open,
a drunk is roaring,
he's lurching and flailing,
the slits of his eyes shed tears.
A shaking form searches for a shape –
is it yours or mine?

You unwrap yourself
clenching your fists,
fragile lines of a half starved body
now curving with muscles,
you grasp his pleading throat.
The fabric of your suit is bursting,

as I add another feather,
a red damask shawl,
a purple line to heighten
the staring blue of my eyes.
This is me now, this is you.
We dance as he multiplies
around us, whistling and cheering.

You awake with a wink
and wrap your arms around me.

## Louise on Darlinghurst Road

Old cynic with his bottle at the bank.
A fine mind thrusts with the darkness,
a swig of brandy to hold the vision,
he sees it just like me –
a grotesque gallery in flux,
sweet kisses and brutishness
passing side by side,
jostling for our future.
A boy sits beside him,
holding a rhinestone,
colours match the flecks in wide open eyes,
as his body quivers
with each detail of the street around us.
I look at it once more,
and remember why I came here,
to glimpse the new
in the blandness
of this meat and potatoes city.

## Vanessa and Tony 3

Our drinks glow blue.
I touch the finely layered weave
of your unbuttoned suit.
A trumpet from the jazz band
sprints invisible steps to triumph.
We're at a table close to the centre,
all around us ties are loosened,
ropes of pearls and jiving shoulders,
lover chases lover, glancing at me and you.
Before you came to the Cross,
you could only dream of this.
Now you're a manager here.
You have a Ford – a streamline – outside,
how it bellows and roars!
You tell me – not so long ago,
you stole them – I did too!
Notes stuff your wallet.
A gorgeous dress adorns me.
I leap to my feet, spinning wildly.
We chart their illicit journeys.

# Refuge For Romantics

Kings Cross, Sydney, 1992

## 1 Helen at the Goldfish Bowl Hotel

Am I rougher than this house wine
in my laddered damask stockings?
In Florence they were beautiful,
like me, but no longer!
How I need a new ghastly shot
just to start my heart again!
Today as I left, you looked away –
was it to hide a shadow
on your scintillating eyes?
Here they sag around me
with pickled whingeing faces,
tearing up their betting slips
or worse –
they tamely flirt and gossip
in their office greys.
Young eyes sparkle,
but so unsubversively!
What has happened to this city?
Were all its juices sucked out
in the years I was away?
A renovation in tiresome white
like sighs in a doctor's waiting room!
I gag a thrill of panic –
Is there a hole in my pocket?

Not even five dollars –
maybe that in change!
Enough for one electric prod of red,
but not enough
even for sweet bubbly
to return to you with flair?
Oh for a Veuve's happy orange label!
But never mind, I can get by!
I've found you a coat
quite unique in striped linen,
I always search as I wander,
only my discriminating eye can spot
a treasure like this at Vinnies!
I want you to wear it.
It'll take you back to livelier days
and give a darker tang
to the wine's cheap sweetness.
I want us to drink
from those delicate crystal tumblers
hand blown by a wizened craftsman
in Perugia's back lanes.
Oh your stories are more fanciful
than mine – and I love you for it!
Just thinking of you
fills my scarred lungs with laughter,
but is that enough to buy me a drink?
Ah I see a friendly face!
His poor young heart
was broken by some brute.

I met him here a week ago,
and turned his saccharine tedious moaning –
that only a pretty rich boy can have –
into whoops of delight!
There he is, walking in a daze!
Charles! Yes! Come in here
for a drink! Come on just one!
Don't be trapped in singular silence!
I can break the barriers!
Let me take you to the bars,
and find you a dimpled boy called Dirk!
But can you lend me twenty dollars?

2

Thank you!
Around us the couples swagger
and seduce, flashing eyes, touching hands.
My venomous darkness brightens!
Doesn't he fascinate – both me and you?
Hands off – have any man – but him!
I've travelled the world – the people
I've met, the turbulent parties!
Then I was back, the Wall had fallen,
everything was pale.
Until I saw the wicked irony
flash in his weary eyes!
He was at the end of his rope,
like me, there was nothing,
just our stories, a few precious baubles,
but it was plenty!

The most loving, the most courageous –
they're dying all around us!
But what a life still throbs in him!
How can he say – like I do –
he's beautiful no longer!
Pah! Not true for him – or for me!
His lines ripple with his laughter,
and his dark shadows shine!
Here's to the ladders in these damask stockings!
Life's too short now for cheap wine!
This will thrill our palates!
Do you have a little more
for pasta, herbs, a can of salmon?
Viola! Let him just wave his hand,
and it'll be a mouth-watering banquet.

## 3 Charles

She took me to their crumbling terrace,
how she found it, I'll never know.
I think it was waiting for demolition,
at a point of transition – like all of us.
Curtains of moth-eaten velvet billow
in the high picture windows, intricate mandalas
flared on mildewed turquoise walls.
A silver candelabra, mottled with grey,
sits with wooden saints and diamante angels
on faded green carpet stained with wine.
Copies of Genet, Rimbaud and Wilde
are scattered on the floor, an oboe's cadences
sing and jump on a funnelled phonogram.

He's wearing a lace shirt with dirty cuffs,
he coos at the linen jacket, and stares at me.
He wants to hear my most passionate
night of sex as we drink from gold-leafed
crystal tumblers, washing down the pasta.
They take me to Berlin, a ribald cabaret
danced to jazz, luscious sailor boys.
They bicker about money
as they improvise a movie
blockbuster, then they turn on me.
I crumple, then they say they love me.
I am always welcome, if I bring some pot,
theirs is a refuge for romantics.
As I leave, the city's rush and traffic
breaks around me and I sigh.

## 4 Helen the Next Morning

As he snores,
I can sense the pain,
his ribcage stretching taut,
expanding and contracting,
breath catching
in knots of phlegm.
I wrap my arms around him,
he's so slight for his thought's wildness!
I'm scared he will awake,
disdainfully
pushing me away.

A flame flickers
from a scarlet stump still molten
in the candelabra.
My brain is tingling
with needles of pain,
I cannot sleep
and do not want to wake.
I trace the texture
of his arm's light hair,
glossing over scars and pockmarks.
The slender warmth
of his muscles flex,
charged with the current
of his stories last night,
backed by the darkness of bass guitar.

I see you now – a young punk dandy,
with spiky purple hair, nose rudely pierced,
looking for the hungry, the dissatisfied.
You could find the right chink
to open any door, a beaten boy
with a drunken father, you travel the world!
Did we fly away in parallel?
I'm reading a fairy tale,
huddled in my room
in a tumbledown house,
crashes and curses shake everything!

I jolt awake, alone with you.
A gold-leafed crystal glass is crushed
between the almost empty bottles.

Just one remaining gulp,
to start my heart again!
Still you snore,
your breath catching,
tufts of chest hair
poke from lace,
your eyebrows shaved,
your reddened lips
torn downwards in a scowl.
What has happened to you?
What has happened to me?
The furrows on my face
are deepening with every hangover.
Florence, London, San Francisco –
all the places we've been,
and our paths never crossed!

I see you lounged in the plushness
of five-star hotel suites,
surrounded by daredevils
walking the cutting edge,
musicians whose chords
tear an audience to frenzy.
Young men are snared
in the gorgeous current of your stories.
I'm pulling beers in back street bars,
pot-bellied men flirt in coloured lights.
Would you have noticed me
back then,
so eager in my awkwardness?

Now you're here, beside me.
Laughter is my only talent.
I cannot write a sentence
without crossing it out,
and my singing
cracks the porcelain in any shower.
Instead I have a gift with people –
I help them to see past their sadness,
I change their pain to wanting.
Here's to the ladders in these damask stockings!

I read your triumphs, see broken teeth
where they've kicked you, kicked me.
You've fallen from grace.
Let me lift you, you bewildering changeling!
There's nothing so enlivening as you!
Can we not build
some startling newness, born of our stories?
Lets start from this crumbling mansion.
What's a little virus?
I'll take it away, and set you free.

# Hospital Dance

to Beverly and Bill Richards

You stare through my wafer of skin –
purple ropes of knotted veins
connect to a mess of wiring,
the rhythm of my heart uneven
in jagged orange lines.
You're holding my hand.
No more pain – just dizziness,
only the greyness of your face is still.

Yet again, the moves are in your eyes –
the bleeping quickens, starts to jive,
you hold me sure, and as I dive,
you pull me in a twisting bounce
to spin on your gyrating thigh,
then up, suspended screaming I glide
over swirling waves of dresses,

landing in the exhilaration of your eyes,
a shower of sweat from flying hair.
You're holding my hand.
Take me home, love, I'm ready.
We're the last ones here,
you see right through to my jumping heart.

## To Nadine

Your voice was high,
over the low hum of your Adam's apple,
I loved your disenchantment.
You served oysters, goats cheese, caviar,
tangy bubbles of Veuve on our tongues
from chipped mugs – 'That horror last week
smashed all my flutes!'
Your slimness quivered with your thoughts
in a finely woven quilted blouse.
We gestured wildly as we built
a man we wanted piece by piece,
mixed race, horse hung, a cello prodigy,
with mischief in his playful eyes…
then a Concorde flight to Paris first class,
to shop for frocks on the Champs Elysée,
or a leather bar with androgynous boys
cracking whips and purring in our arms
in Berlin as the brownshirts hover.
'They never go away, pet. Only the costumes change!'
We'd kick a politician in his hairy eyebrows,
take a bland conniving businessman,
truss him up in leather straps…
then suddenly stop and sigh.
Sarti shimmers on your gramophone,
you're twisting your fingers in a ball,
your voice seethes in all its layers –
'This city is so beige,
lets go and paint it red.'

We'd drain a last drop from the bottles
and flounce together for the mirror,
hesitate, then flounce again.
Lets reshape the world with glamorous lies.

2

The music thumps
My head revolves,
I see your face
in green, then blue, then sickly green,
the others hiding themselves away from me.
I'm in agitation
of seeking – of not belonging,
then it all repeats again.
A punch is thrown,
then your arms are gyrating
wildly in the oscillating light,
you're spinning in a panic.
I wrap myself around you,
your body spasms,
to hit out aimless in its frailty,
I reel from a punch, meant for you –
I do not offend them.

Outside now, safe,
you're sobbing as I sit in silence.
You're in a place
I'm just a push away from,
a place I never let myself go.

Nearby is the door.
They're entering and leaving
with their guarded nonchalance,
unapproachable, beige, what is there to know?
You gather yourself, as if to resist,
'You see what it's like to be me.'
'And me too.'
A passerby laughs.
Where can we go?
I want to run away.

3

All I have now is your drawing –
your nervous tension,
a reflection of mine
tightly unfurling
in red and black lines.
A gorgeously femme hermaphrodite,
flying strands of floating hair.
The eyes in shadows
ever deepened by your restless pencil,
hurting but ready to fight,
staring outwards,
This is me.
Your passion changed laws
to end transsexual hate speech.
You're standing firm.
We stumbled together to find our own way.
You start to split apart, lurching drunk from a bar.
They laughed at you.

Sometimes I did too.
One more push and that's where I'd be.
You turned your passion in on yourself.

4

This city is beiger without you.
Darlinghurst Road is silent at dusk,
shaking with my coffee fumes.
I hear your voice,
its many layers shriller than before.
You fantasise, bathed in neon lights.
I twist my fingers in a ball,
and feel a little of your fury.

# Maria Barbola

from Velasquez, *las Meininas*, Royal Palace, Madrid, 1656

Maria, you mirror the delicate Princess,
woman with a man's broad face,
body like a brawling boy
now restrained in a velvet gown,
no taller than she twisting
to catch your waiting eyes,
as a dog stirs at your feet.
She's poised to break away,
laughter ripples the frozen composure
of her glowing white dress,
the dog leaps,
licking her face as she cuddles him.
You strike a goblin's pose
as she leaps on your back, shrieking…
…I find the moment
when the Princess bored
by her ladies' deference
looks within and beyond
the vaulted splendour of the chamber,
like you, Maria
both free to spark
a moment of disorder
as the dog yawns, then awakens.

Maria you can mould yourself
to a parody of the oiliest supplicant,
curtsy like a duchess, threaten like a thug,
pluck a mandolin
to sing of your forever unrequited love,
you contain it all
in the freakish pliability of your body.
But you are nothing
without the echo of laughter
shaking their silken robes
or your backward somersault
as you gleefully recoil from a kick.
The only clue
is the knowing distance in your eyes,
the tense resignation of your mouth,
as free as a princess,
but just as restrained.

As I paint
a trumpet sounds
no doubt an ambassador
bejewelled with orders,
marches to the presence of the king.
Soldiers in scarlet
hold the sumptuous fabric
of his lady's train aloft.
That is their concern, Maria.

We strove all our lives to reach this palace,
to reflect its glowing tension back,
to be dismissed with a wave
if that is their wish.
We are both in the painting for now,
forever if I get it right.
We say little as we drink
from goblets emblazoned with royal arms.
When you leave
I start to find the secret of your face.

# Martin's Painting

Jim.
You travel the world,
while I sit here.
You never change, naughty and elfin.
You now pour as the roast crackles.
The candles flicker as we laugh.
We hear an echo – another breath
is buoying our mirth – a sudden peel
of pure joyful anarchy – is it you, Martin?
We pick up our glasses and turn.
Are your lips flat? No – they're poising
with fullness. The muscles in your forearm
flex. Your glass is toasting us! Your body shapely,
bathed in deep blue thoughtfulness, your eyes closed.
You sit apart, alive to the moment, cheeks colouring
like a debutante, shy of our gaze.
You're waiting…to laugh again, relishing
the quirky contrast of Jim and me?
Suddenly we hug– we know why we're here.
Your likeness as a woman hangs on my wall,
a moment of your fantasy, so often forgotten,
following me for twenty years. Now I realise –
in unconscious yearning, I've placed the candles,
cooked the same roast, dusted the painting,
so you and I can find the gateway to…

…the candelabra reaches for the roof
and glows. 'I'm Martin – no – Janice.
Clarissa?' 'Just call me Charles.
I saw you when I heard your laugh.'

Now you're quiet. Can I touch your thoughts?
They're prancing lovable
their tongues barbed, plumage
textured like exotic birds,
telling their ribald stories…
There you are, Jim – cigarette red raw,
dressed as a whore. But Martin – you sit apart,
bathed in blue, cheeks colouring, shying from gazes.
I'm Mrs Dalloway, gentle and refined
full of secret fantasies my mask can't hide.
Are you amazed? Like me…
At this drunken cacophony, men as women,
women as drag queens, carving roast meat,
as someone vomits under the table?
The room expands, the focus shifts,
from deep hewn eyes sparkling,
to the warmth of each eccentric face,
taking us on their taunting journey,
and like me, looking for the key to you.
Have you stumbled here, sensing you belong,
to escape the rushing overpriced blandness
of the city outside? I watch you,
lips poising full, finding fuel for
the wonder of your laugh. New shapes
are beckoning, vivid from the life around us.
Like me kissing you? Now is not the time,
our thoughts grow in parallel.
Your eyes close, searching out your need.
Was it that night?
You promised me a painting…

Jim? Jim? Are you OK?
Our talking stops.
We look at the picture, back to each other.
You called me one day.
Martin is dead.
You'd found him, shivering and frightened,
gasping with pneumonia. They couldn't save him.
You travel the world, and I sit here.
Mrs Dalloway. Juggling my fantasies.
We're ever more quirky. So stubbornly
single.
We raise our glasses.

# Silver Birch Tree in China

inspired by a painting by James Withington

I stare at the skin of a silver tree,
as people stream around, gleaming in ordered chaos,
passing so close they displace the smoky air.
A few heads twist with a sideways step

around the crazy foreigner,
notebook in hand, totally fascinated
with the oh so familiar, as if it's a miracle –
the trunk of a tree like all the others,

neatly fixed in a long row. The traffic honks,
living dangerously, as bicycles
weave and pedestrians scurry,
it's all so fast, I can see only this…

A wide open eye with crows feet,
reflecting the gaze of a middle-aged traveller.
A stare from the sheen of silvery bark
stitched with black diamonds
and spoked wheels poised to spin again…

Is it only cold sap? Piercing the tissue
like black ink from the pen of an etcher
working deep inside, scarring with his infinite patience.

Cuts cluster and fatten into lashes around
an unblinking eye. Are they random blemishes,
growing more grotesque with the passing years?
Incongruous with the faces flashing by

in colourful fabrics, the glowing pastel
of the latest mobile phones,
and none of them pause to see what I see,
but speed past full of purpose in continuous blur.

I stand confused, a tourist here for a day,
perhaps a week, my head revolving
as I stare at the frenetic city around me,
then a story emerging from the bark's surface.

I see monkeys playing beneath a jungle canopy,
apples fall on their heads, and a praying mantis
is poised with poisonous claws
to catch an insect it can never reach.

The eyes soften, now laughing as long as the tree
keeps growing. Millimetre by millimetre
year by year, the ink flows, sap welling
drop by drop, congealing in canny observation.

A Cyclops clown is pedaling a unicycle,
fixed to the spot. He etches with satiric glee
the gleaming throngs, circling daily to perpetuity.
I pick up my charcoal to capture the shapes…

Eyes are dreaming in bodies rushing forward.
Cartwheeling children leap around and laugh.
A woman seductively eats an apple,
as a young man follows, his arms outstretched.

I move from tree to tree, the pattern shifts
with ever wilder variation. I'm here for a day,
perhaps a week. They laugh at me,
incongruous, a crazy foreigner sketching
blemishes on a tree. Ink flows
on silver bark as the tree grows.

# 2014

### Seven years old near Kerri Kerri, New Zealand, 1971

I'm looking high above me.
He's a dressing gown striped
black and blue like night falling –
no more tumbling playfulness.
Red prints of fox-hunters leap,
the Queen is beaming young,
light bulbs shine through diamonds
streaked with colours, like some fable.
Two sticks
press on a flat line of roses
so slowly,
I circle and jump
asking questions
he doesn't answer, till I feel
my father's hand and stop.
A polished oak table,
his face is a shadow,
we all quiver with his pain
as he lowers to his chair,
only then can we sit.
Not that fork, that one,
don't talk with your mouth full,
or you'll go to your room,
He's sitting silent, as a roast waits
in a bewildering chorus of voices.
The patterns on his silver knife glow
as he places the meat on his fork,
lifting it so delicately.
He's my grandfather,
and I try to eat like him…

## A small flat in Potts Point, Sydney, 2014

…I'm sitting at my desk,
stirring fragments of a different age.
My grandfather doubles over,
a cough is shattering his frailty.
I open a faded scarlet book,
the title in gold lettering
framed with Roman columns.
*Brave Deeds for British Boys.*
I found it at a jumble sale.
*Its purpose –*
*to rouse in its readers*
*a longing*
*for courage and heroism.*
*To say with all your heart*
*as you read it*
*I want to rise to the height of heroism,*
*to do my duty*
*at all costs*
*against all hazards.*
Pages are turning to brown and falling.
Magill Methodist College 1902,
*to* – name crossed out – *for Punctuality.*
Did he believe it?
Did he die?
Troops scuttle jerkily in black and white,
the bell is tolling,
fifty thousand dying like cattle
for a mile of cratered mud.

Crowds cheer wildly waving flags,
war is declared, do I sweep forward,
or stand back,
scorched with white feathers?
Lord Kitchener's face,
moustache like Stalin,
eating up the young,
'I want you!'
as Mahler's layered oboes yearn,
an adagio in Vienna – 1913…
when suddenly
out of trembling words
I see my reflection.
He's laughing in colour
running towards me,
my brother.
He obliterates the shadows,
the explosions close by of sudden death,
*wherever he went, he brought happiness*,
for a moment, I'm my grandfather.
What did he mean?
Did he say that, my grandfather?
I'm at my desk staring into space,
with Wilfred Owen, a history of the war,
*Brave Deeds*, as Mahler still plays,
images drift, but cannot catch,
until again…

Two men embrace and laugh
against the wreckage of a landscape,
one of them very soon to die,
the other my grandfather.
*I met him by chance.*
*It was* – did he say – *beautiful?*
Whose words are those?
My grandfather's? Mine?
*The last time I met him.*
*He was the best of us.*
*My favourite brother.*
A face like my own
speaks to a figment.
They fade to a blurred dance of colour,
then nothing.
I pick up my pen and start to write.

## from the Biography of General Sir Bernard Freyberg, VC, KG, DSO (three bars) Governor-General of New Zealand 1948–54

*Four brothers. A fighting family.*
*I embraced the war with all my heart.*
*Cuthbert* (my grandfather) *an airman…gassed…shot down…*
*wounded several times…twice mentioned in dispatches…*
*Oscar was killed at Gallipoli in 1915.*
*Paul joined as a rifleman in 1916. He died of his wounds at*
*Messines in 1917.*
Your brothers joined as soon as they could, but you joined later, Paul. As a private, not as an officer like your brothers. Why?

## At my desk, Potts Point

What did he tell me, my grandfather?
When?
Grandpa and Paul:
brothers, officer and private,
meeting by chance,
on leave behind the lines,
a building pierced with shell holes,
full of drunken frightened soldiers,
what did they say?
I probe and it recedes,
flickering with rats, barbed wire,
the smug poison of the book,
I cannot embroider further
from my safe and peaceful life
except this loop of images anyone
who reads can conjure.
Yet I still see this chimera,
sparked by trembling words
fading away as I try to remember.
Who can I ask – I want to know!
My father's sipping good red
listening to Mahler, Beethoven,
nodding in his armchair,
so tatty and worn without him…
My uncle Peter gone, Kitty –
Communist, gardener, family historian gone –
I never asked when I had the chance.
I email my cousins who I hardly see.

*He never ever talked about the war!*
Really?
Was this about the war?
Or about Paul calling his name,
*bringing happiness to everyone he met*
just before he died.
My grandpa's story…

## *The Dominion* newspaper, Wellington, 27 June 1917

*Paul Freyberg, a young man 33 years of age who stood 6'2'*
*The news of his death in action was received this morning.*
*He worked as a law clerk.*
*He was a young man of high ideals,*
*With a bright disposition that made him friends everywhere.*
*He was an enthusiastic yachtsman, courageous at the tiller.*
*He wrote verses, and interesting articles for New Zealand*
*Yachtsman, under the soubriquet Boat 'Arbour Bill.*
*He headed the movement to plant trees at Ward Island.*
*He will be sorely missed.*

## Darlinghurst Road, Kings Cross, Sydney, 1991

They were dangerous times. I was awaiting the results of
my aids test. I was walking home from the pick-up bars of
Oxford St, drunk, alone. I heard him call my name. He
was running towards me wheezing, breathless, in danger of
falling in a hospital smock and bracelet – I wrapped my arms
around him. In the glaring neon, I could see how sick he was.
His skin was blotchy, almost transparent, stretched across the
bones of his face. His blue eyes sparkled crazy.

'Lets go for a drink.'
'You need to go back to hospital.'
'I'm never going back there.'

So we went for a drink. I can't remember what we talked about, just the trembling urgency of his voice. Eventually I coaxed him into a cab and back to the hospice.

He was such a rebel. He enlivened everyone he met. It was the last time I saw him. The meeting shocked me so deeply.

In the late 80s and early 90s, one in five gay men were infected with HIV. So many of them died. The same casualty rate as the young men fighting in World War I.

## Kerri Kerri, New Zealand, Summer, 1971

My father high dived from a rock
into the deep green pool.
I was frightened, but I followed him –
what a thrill when I first did it!
We flew over on a plane – just two weeks a year!
A grey horse's breath as he lowers his head
and nuzzles me, he is my friend.
My grandmother ties smelly saddle straps,
I'm grabbing his mane, screaming and bouncing,
following her through explosive green,
we gather ripe oranges from her orchard.
I'm snuggling in lace as she tells me stories,
Mowgli again and again, the Queen of Hearts.
She called England home,
but she never went there.
I adored her, she adored me.
Then I went to sit with grandpa…

From *The New Zealand Yachtsman*, 10 June, 1916

*Life Aboard a Troop Ship*
By Paul Freyberg, writing as Boat 'Arbour Bill

*We are in the Great Australian Bight.*
*Our little hooker, though a twin screw, is scarcely three thousand tonnes.*
*Down in the hold are long tiers of bunks, dignified by the name of dormitories, with dormitory sergeants to chase the men up.*
*For misdemeanours, there is the stokehold.*
*Parades are held at different times, we do our drills and sophomores.*
*Light out strictly at 9 p.m. I was wedged in my bunk.*
*We ran into a fierce squall.*
*I couldn't resist putting on an overcoat, and jumping up on deck to see how she was taking it.*
*The sea was lashed into white foam by the hail and sleet.*
*She lifted to the seas in splendid style, then down, down into the trough she went, until the foredeck was nearly level with the water.*
*Up without a pause, reaching the summit of the next wave.*
*To the yachtsman, the trip is a splendid one, he enjoys every minute, revelling in rough weather when parades are cut out.*

## My Grandfather's Bedroom

My feet don't touch the ground,
the chair purple velvet
softer than my horses' face.
He's wrapped up in shadow
on a great oak bed.
My hair still wet from swimming,
I've skipped in from sunshine,
still fluttering through heavy drapes
with splashes of breeze.
A cigarette's point flares orange,
his cough explodes, then fingers shaking
a striped handkerchief.
'You sat with him for hours!' my mother now tells me.
'We left you alone. We never saw you so quiet.'
My words are now, the images then,
the image a word not said to a child,
but I understood…
Sheets knot in greyness, his flattened height
twisting towards me – he was more astonishing
than diving high from a rock into water,
or rolling down a hill and feeling sick.
His face leans closer as my eyes adjust,
delicate silk stained with purple,
almost transparent,
showing veins like worms.
Fine lines swirl and furrow into contours,
immobile like a mask pierced with blue eyes.
The smell of stale tobacco, perfume of powder.

His voice trembled low, words slow as his walk.
He stares as his thoughts wrap around me,
his memories quiver from the shadows.
The child's image merges with his brother.

## *History of the New Zealand Rifle Brigade* by Lt-Col. W.S. Austin
## 17 June 1917 – the night of Paul's death

*Night attack launched at 9 p.m.*
*German aircraft reconnoitre*
*An intense bombardment opened up on the trenches.*
*Advance in darkness a leap into the unknown.*
*Area swept by enemy machine guns and artillery.*
*Neither commanders nor men failed.*
*This night witnessed counterattack work of the highest order.*
*By skilful flank work, we drove the enemy out.*
*On the vantage point, we established a line of snipers.*

## Paul's Photo

He stands in his uniform
Awkward
He's elsewhere
like I so often am.
He's my height – and his face…
It's mine.

# The Tickle

Shostakovitch's Piano Quintet in G minor Movement 3 translated to words

Your panting is precocious,
you reek perfume and vodka.
You've discovered me
hidden in my cupboard
a discarded toy
tightly wound.
Your fingers,
so superbly trained,
pluck under my arms
at taut nerves.
You do not stop,
next you're pinching my nipples
opening a forgotten cluster
of throbbing neurons,
my limbs are thrashing sharply.
I am squirming
pinned to the ground
watching your muscles flex
rhythmic with my howls
now deepening to chuckles.
For a moment you soften,
I beam with your caress.
Then you attack,
tickling me some more.

# A Taunting Question in His Eyes…

1

Like the acid fruit
of the bottle's last glass,
a taunting question in his eyes
blows past us in the breeze,
I blush at his joke, then laugh.
I glance at you, asking you again –
you've known him for longer –
'What can we do about him?
Did we do enough…'
I add another piece
to your portrait of him,
a ribbon tying back
his long flowing hair, and…
I break off my sentence,
then as I raise my fork,
tangy flesh pungent with nuts and chilli,
he's almost with us,
it's like a taste of him!
Together we gather a collage around him,
a throw of purple velvet,
wilting orchids in gold-leafed china,
a broken doll wrapped in barbed wire,
he caresses a sequined cushion
as he describes some lover begging.
Can a morsel of risotto soothe
a wrecked liver,
a body attacking itself?

He pauses frail, playing with worry beads,
hilarity bursting from reddened eyes.
I order another bottle,
smiling at the slimness of a dark haired waiter,
striding lively towards us,
I want to pinch his bottom –
just as he would have done.
Around us, well dressed couples
tinkle and coo politely,
he's truly gone, with all his outrageous
infuriating playfulness…

## 2 Your story – a St Kilda night thirty years ago

Four o'clock in the morning,
one last martini.
He's near but unreachable,
surrounded by muscles in leather,
purple bobs, glistening eyes,
dark rhythms of chaos barely restrained,
the leap and thump of dancing feet.
He stands near the centre,
absorbing and reflecting,
lace shirt and cape,
his nose rudely pierced,
an upending of fashion
on his graceful form,
everyone is watching.

I push close to listen,
but he moves so swiftly...
to a tattooed bruised looking man,
maybe fresh out of prison,
adoring eyes glance from rough stubble,
just one of his followers, women and men.
It was different back then.
Caution fled to hide in the suburbs,
the mansions were crumbling,
paint peeling from grafittied walls.
Wealth was in the moment's energy,
the endless search of guitar and song.
People were dying, one needle they're gone,
in the midst of bursting youthful resonance.
This world was new to me and it shocked,
I wanted to understand,
it was full of ugly incoherence,
but when I stood with him and saw through his eyes...
He told his stories – of a beaten boy,
wrapping himself in the jostling elements,
writing it large with wild imagination,
burning a hole through the yawn, the cliché,
all the trash that oppresses.
I had my camera...
I wanted it to flow in images,
what he saw, I saw...
Next day in a studio,
a young man sings a love song,
bloody hands holding a rose,
while prisoners dance and purple-haired vamps
cracking whips ride in on Harleys.

We travel the world,
flying away on his fancies.
I add the missing brush strokes,
the right light and colour.
Whatever his wildness, or his quietness,
I strove to enhance, and protect.
Until the end…

## 3 My story – twenty years later

A silk shirt with velvet collar
hangs loosely
around panting ribs.
He's impeccable as always.
His eyes glow wide,
against cheekbones tightly stretched
with blotched grey flesh.
Does he note my kiss?
I ask him how he feels.
He laughs disdainfully.
'You drift through life,
your senses blunt,
without the spice of pain.'
I follow his stare
into leaves shaking in the breeze,
seeing them now with his fascination.
He's holding a quill.
An angel boy wrestles a gargoyle –
a rape in Indian ink.
I blush then laugh.

He always moves pain
to a startling hilarity.
The dullness of my daily static,
tiredness from work,
some unreturned phone call,
changes to the wildness of wanting.
Other wheelchairs gather around us,
pinched faces open –
he's the hospice clown.
Hour later when I leave
bursting with energy,
I hasten to a nearby bar,
to harmonise my thoughts,
to find a man.

4

What now then for you?
Your blue eyes are exploring…
As young drunks wander in circles,
scattering their tension,
below bleached white balconies
with floor to ceiling blinded windows.
When I find new friendships,
there's something of his abrasiveness,
the daring shine of his eyes,
taking me beyond the daily static.
You smile knowingly.

We separate once more
to homes in different cities
newly enlivened
to continue our searching,
until we meet again
to conjure him between us.

# Bruise

Young in London 1986

You're standing on the edge drinking lager.
*He* stands near the centre, swaying to music
I start to like now, seeing electric potential
in the muscles tightly flexing in his shirt.
A sinew twitches, moving up the base of his thumb
as he touches a shoulder beside him
and his teeth bare quickly in a grin.
You are not watching him. I think like me
you came to this bar alone, and like me
you don't know quite how to be here.
So your questioning face, upraised a little
acknowledging me there delights me.
You giggle in girlish cockney.
I see you're even younger than me.
Then – a stain of purple
fed by blood. Sarcoma
under peachy fuzz…
I can't stop seeing…
How it seeps hurt more than any punch,
but at the same time
liking the urgency of your eyes,
and the pitch of your voice,
its warm emotion cutting through
the beat and grunts of talk behind.
Your cigarette shakes from twig like arms,
your coat hangs off you like a drunk's blanket,
your shoulders filled it once – and I know
it's running in you out of control, it can't be hidden.

I bend to catch your breath,
your words now soft, questioning.
You see what's in me,
standing out in purple like your bruise,
the drive to be wanted tonight,
you feel it too – more than ever.
I whisper in your ear about the coldness
I can't stop feeling between the imposing buildings,
the teeming crowds, writing home, writing my thoughts
in a tiny room booming with traffic, then walking out…
You tell me of a man – you don't know where he is.
You were sick, but now you're getting better…
Then we try to keep it light, but there's too much
behind your eyes, as we swivel and gesture and
run out of words, I turn away from you and look at him.
*His* eyes steady and twinkling, reflecting all the others
who twist and stare at him, but he looks beyond.
I want to wear his thoughtless ease,
to give the thrill he does when he touches,
but he doesn't see me, so I look back at you.
And I wish I had the spell to send
this curse too frightening to even name
away – and make you like him, but still like you.
You'd keep the flashing in your eyes,
and he'd find the dark singing in your voice.
But I only find this thought too late,
walking in the dark of a windy street,
knowing I'm part of this city's cruelty.

# Oberon

## 1 Home

The bed is torn with insomnia,
colourful sheets knotted brightly,
twisted at random and empty,
exposing the old stained mattress.
Two glasses
both blotted with the same redness,
one still standing,
the other is fallen on dirty green carpet.
We held them together
not last night,
was it the night before?
Not this hangover anyway.
Greasy plates from our last dinner
are festering in the sink.
Little reminders of your provoking chaos
are everywhere.
'Ill met by moonlight, proud Titania.'
There I stop,
and take in my hand a little flower
purple with love's wound –
is there still just a smudge of makeup,
a blossom in my hair?
Suddenly I see you,
strangely quiet beside me.
I fill your glass,
and kiss around your freckled cheek.

Fragrant, you laugh and push me away,
then take me in your arms,
a single kiss, a stare, a sneer,
when leaping up, you scatter the moment.
As you dance,
in circles wide and wilder,
I mirror you within,
watching you unsweetly mouth
some love song's airbrushed words,
and stumble in a pirouette
that dazzles with your anger.
Now we're poised in utter stillness,
just reaching with our breath.
Your eyes appeal,
then thrill to my stare.
I now leap…
…but you're gone.
Now everything is silent,
except for…
As I stand my arms move out
as wide as a flowering forest,
darkened with nooks of savage sensuality,
and rising trills of fairies laughing,
supporting the thrill,
the spite of Shakespeare's language.
I mouth half a speech,
but it shrivels in a sigh,
a whinge – nothing like the fairy king…

My arms embrace again,
your breathing body fills
the twist of colourful sheets,
but I know the bed is empty…
It's still so far to eight o'clock,
the floodlit gardens,
where everything resolves,
and I know the pang of all this
can enliven the moment…
or tear apart my performance.

## 2 Theatre

They wonder at love's elusiveness
as they enter the enchanted forest –
*swift as a shadow, short as any dream,*
*brief as lightening in the coiled night,*
*that in a spleen, unfolds both heaven and earth…*
I'm muttering words so explosive and right,
applying more perfumed blush to my cheek,
teasing in wax the wildness of my hair,
wrapping blossoms into the strands.
It's a small room, dull with fluoro light,
a fellow actor shakes and hums,
bags are scattered, magazines half read.
I'm quivering with appalling stage-fright,
recalling discoveries, the moments I leap,
a line long flat, but last night suddenly
it sizzled with meaning, but how? What?

My arms spread as wide as the flowering forest,
and the defiance in Titania's face
starts mingling with your succulent freckles.
I taste my power in a flower's purple stain,
to humiliate her, to make you writhe.
Puck knows, we giggle in our complicity.
The door opens, the stage manager smiles,
blinding glare of lights, shadows of trees,
garlands of flowers, the fabric of my cape flares out,
and you stand there, after your pirouette,
breathing in stillness, about to leap again.
'Ill met by moonlight, proud Titania!'

## 3 Pub

'You were good tonight.' It's Titania.
'No, really good. You frightened me.'
I am deliciously empty, holding a beer.
Her boyfriend is beside her, cheerful and friendly.
He comes to see her every night,
but I couldn't see you,
as I anxiously scanned the applauding audience.
'Except,' she says, 'I can see he's hurting you.
Isn't it time to…' 'Yes, I agree.'
And as I say it, I see you awkwardly
glowing the first time I kissed you.
My voice cracked as I asked you some question,
your prickly wildness melted my reserve,
and I followed you out, shaking with excitement.

I could eat her boyfriend for breakfast,
and still need more. What do I want?
'Another beer?' I ask them.

## 4 Later – a Nightclub

Is this where you found him?
Last night?
Some ass sweetly mouthing
the airbrushed words of a love song?
Did his body seem shapely,
the flaws washed away
in the coloured flash of lights,
like the purple juice
of a flower in your eye?
Or did he glimpse you,
the leanness of your shadow
poised to leap?
Well I can find that moment too!
Together the crowd pulsates,
waving arms and coloured torsos,
one energy jumping
in plumes of smoke
fluorescent like a lost sea creature
thrashing to the surface.
If only I could be entangled
and lose this painful oneness!
No – let this woundedness swell
more strident, fuelled by this drink!

The king of the fairies
stripped of his billowing cape,
cruising here incognito,
a parade gyrating, ever shifting, deaf
to explosively textured monologues.
She said I was good. Titania!
You'd have liked me too,
but it's over with you, over
if it ever really even started!
My needfulness finds rhythm,
the tension of it reflects around me,
What's your story, handsome stranger?
Can I lose myself in the sadness of your eyes?
I breath in, but can say nothing.
How can you really seize another?

## 5 Walking Home

Can I gather
walking home
legs exhausted
the words to make you see?
Where's my strength to shake?
Breathing in and out
there's only clouds of smoke.
Can I gather
the weight
of this never-ending night
into the shining
energy of the play's gorgeous words?

I cannot remember them.
Nothing matters.
Except –
In the windy darkness of this street,
is our light on?
I rehearse bitter words,
but my legs are running.
My body is tingling with reproach.
The door opens,
you take me in your arms.
A laugh, a single kiss, a sneer…

# To an Old Friend

## 1 A couple of years ago

Alone with you,
I want to walk away,
and realise – now I can.
I heard your voice
still mocking the intercom
with its surreal challenge.
Now your laughter ricochets
with a congested rasp,
twisting a now habitual scowl
to the warmth of your anarchy.
I play hard ball.
'You've exploded –
all that's left are the pieces,
to be picked up with gloved hands
and burning tongs
for the body bag.'
I knew you'd like it
in your rich perversity.
It's your kind of joke,
now I'm making it.
'Like father, like son,'
but you say it blearily,
much too slow off the mark,
and I agree.
Then I demand you leave.
'You're drunk!'
'Relax – it's only one or two.'

'And the rest. It's destroyed you.
I can't stand it.'
You pick yourself up,
hinges squeaking,
dressed like a scarecrow,
the frays in your dirty
punk suit top
let in a freezing wind
that almost topples you.
But you stand at full height
to prove your sobriety,
eyes mad with venom,
twitching lips seeking a curse,
until the greyness of your face
softens
familiar again
pleadingly playful.
I look away.
'I made you.'
I don't budge,
and hear your uneven steps
echo down to nothing
in the corridor.

## 2 Over twenty years before. London

Alone with you,
I want to walk away,
but I can't.
Your long fingers
keep rhythm with your words,
gently caressing some purring cat
I cannot see.
You burnt my law books.
You blot out feeble kisses
from men who look away,
their primal passion spent.
My mother's duffel coat and plain check shirt
seem puny, swamped
by your black cloak billowing,
rouge lips and fine peroxide curls.
You unsmother me.
Books crushed by scholarly nail biting
are live bombs in your hands.
It is midnight, and you are resonant.
We wander like lost souls from Becket,
my voice rises higher in step
with yours as we glow.
Our breath condenses to fog
tinged with yellow. We shiver,
weighed down by the polished stone
of massive buildings. Mindless wealth
replicates around us, it sneers and chants,
you bite back with gleeful parody,
and I do too, a faltering reflection,

clenched with vertigo on the edge with you.
What little that's left of me mixes
with the sharpness of your figments –
of Rimbaud bursting between us
shouting '*merde*', with Jimmy vicious
as he rides the storm with Oscar
in the turquoise walls of Reading Gaol,
that crumble to nothing as you
suddenly scowl at me…
You are infectious, you are poisonous,
we are outsiders,
a place I can only be with you.
You wildly point above –
I see nothing. You point again –
at branches faint shadows against the rainbow
glow of streetlights, and the dark blue
of the sky as it reflects the incandescence
of this endless city. High above our heads,
these branches sharpen in focus,
stabbing out leafless twigs
at random angles, multiplying to the tension
of a web where every pattern breaks,
like tentacles drawing us
into their complexity.
There are no rules, only this.
I look down
and watch it all shiver through your body.
You are shedding tears,
your eyes boiling
like blue egg yolks.

You stare at me
like you want to drink my blood.
Are you frightened?
I stare back and suddenly
you soften to your warm anarchy,
pleading and playful.
I see you're me,
blundering to new insights.
I want you to look at me.
My body is pulsating, and I want
to offer you all of my excitement,
every shred of it, sensing my beauty.
I want to hold you.
I can never go back.
Your laughter ricochets.
You look back up and stare.

## Chick Corea's Crimson Sun in Brunswick

The spines in your bookshelf
grow flesh and are alive –
always moving back and forth.
Every day your elbows rest
like mine do now
on the scratched walnut armrests
of this tatty armchair.
Intriguing names beckon
offering to absorb and intimidate –
poets waiting for me
all my life.
My mind is wandering
in parallel with yours,
shimmering then quickening
in the languid summer heat
up and down a jazz piano
like Chick Corea playing –
I'm sampling your vinyl too.
I follow the stepping stones
of your thoughtfulness,
gingerly turning pages
so your brightly coloured markers
do not flutter to the floor.
Discarded beside me,
a Parisian intellectual
for later,
much too dense to digest just now.

You knew I'd like Manhattan's streets
screeching
as a poet in his bedroom basks,
his pick-up just departed.
What now for me?
The question burning
as I flew down –
Sydney couldn't answer,
didn't care.
When I looked into your room
your head was high
as you typed with determined grimace.
You want to capture
in your sentences
the nuance
of urban poets overbalancing
in the density of their seeing.
Of course you can!
But me…
I cannot focus.
My thoughts are sparking,
flowing free
but then evaporating
like my sweat
on this sultry afternoon.
A character I can't write
suddenly shouts
you must
write me!

He's faster than Chick Corea,
with the thoughtful lust
of a Manhattan poet,
Parisian precocious…
Then you walk in,
floating in the paradox
of a freshly finished paragraph.
It's your smile
that holds you to the ground.
Together we open our mouths to speak,
but there's too much in our heads, so
you turn, looking out the window!
The skies are grey,
not just with clouds –
smoke floats, like a gauze
on gaps of dirty blue.
A small bright ball is falling–
surely not the sun!
We can stare
at liquefied crimson,
tearing beneath its surface,
smudged with the haze
of distant fires burning.
Is the world ending?
We remember dire predictions.

Houses are burning
we don't know where,
and suddenly the urgency
of our never ending questioning,
takes on a clearer form,
enlivened by danger around us.
What now for you?
What now for me?
For all our cloistered speculations?
The multicoloured iron of Brunswick roofs
ripple with the notes of Chick Corea,
rusted red, then blue with yellow stripes,
glowing with crimson.
'Let's go for a drink.'
On the street the trams clatter,
headscarves next to hippies,
no one look is normal.
Night has fallen.
Your books reappear,
questioned by a crimson sun.

# Pick Up

Were your eyes asking
across the bar?
Others circle in clusters,
looking round and through me.
A gleam again
as I approach,
the wildness of your curls
pretty as a lost minstrel.
The faraway painting of a bar
leaps to life around you
like an electric shock.
I read my night's kaleidoscope of wanting
in your pause,
coiled in stillness,
resisting the relentless beat.
I try to find a question
but words
my subtle building blocks
drain of all meaning
except as breath
tickling and reddening your cheek.
Did you move closer?
I wait for you to move again,
so my body
now struck dumb
can start to speak.

I touch your back
and suddenly
your body kicks
your kiss a blow
my kiss can't soothe
inflaming tongues hands
I'm lost in you...

In the street
it's like you don't know me,
you're floating
away from the shouts
and rushing cars.
Your eyes are distant
in their early morning blue.
My thoughts writhe,
like a captured animal
in a box beside us.
Your lips relax,
then falter,
searching for a note
you've almost forgotten.
You stare but do not smile,
fingers running on my back.
You want.
Much more than you can say.
Our lips lightly hesitate,
tongues touch.
I push you against
a laneway wall.

Charles Freyberg is a Kings Cross (Sydney) poet and playwright. In the 1990s he worked as an actor and director, especially with the surreal clown Victor Sheehan, his first poetic mentor. His own writing began with his performance art staged at Club Bent at the Performance Space in the late nineties, and with a number of plays. He studied poetry at postgraduate level at the University of Sydney, supervised by Judith Beveridge. His poems have been published in *Meanjin* and *Plumwood Mountain*. Parts of 'Chelsea Manning' and 'Reflexivity' were performed in *the Experiment* by Peter Urquhart at the Sydney Conservatorium. He performs his work widely around Sydney. He gives thanks to the beautiful enlivening eccentrics who have inspired him.

www.ingramcontent.com/pod-product-compliance
Lightning Source LLC
Chambersburg PA
CBHW070922080526
44589CB00013B/1395